I0407966

Contents

How Preferential Trade Agreements Affect the U.S. Economy

Summary

Preferential trade agreements (PTAs) are treaties that remove barriers to trade and set rules for international commerce between two countries or among a small group of countries. PTAs directly affect a country's economy by altering its flows of trade and investment. Primarily through trade, PTAs indirectly affect other aspects of a country's economy—such as productivity, output, and employment. As of August 2016, the United States had established 14 PTAs with 20 of its trading partners. This report examines the economic literature on trade and PTAs and summarizes that literature's findings on how trade and PTAs have affected the U.S. economy.

How Does Trade Affect the U.S. Economy?

International trade yields several benefits for the U.S. economy. Trade increases competition between foreign and domestic producers. That increase in competition causes the least productive U.S. businesses and industries to shrink; it also enables the most productive businesses and industries in the United States to expand to take advantage of profitable new opportunities to sell abroad and obtain cost savings from greater economies of scale. As a result, trade encourages a more efficient allocation of resources in the economy and raises the average productivity of businesses and industries in the United States. Through that increase in productivity, trade can boost economic output and workers' average real (inflation-adjusted) wage. In addition, U.S. consumers and businesses benefit because trade lowers prices for some goods and services and increases the variety of products available for purchase.

Not everyone benefits from trade expansion, however. Although increases in trade probably do not significantly affect total employment, trade can affect different workers in different ways. Workers in occupations, businesses, and industries that expand because of trade may make more money, whereas workers in occupations, businesses, and industries that shrink may make less money or experience longer-than-average unemployment. Such losses can be temporary or permanent. Nevertheless, economic theory and historical evidence suggest that the diffuse and long-term benefits of international trade have outweighed the concentrated short-term costs. That conclusion has consistently received strong support from the economics profession.[1]

Why Does the United States Establish Preferential Trade Agreements?

The United States establishes preferential trade agreements for economic and noneconomic reasons. Those agreements enable the United States and its partner countries to realize the economic benefits of increased trade and investment. In addition, the agreements sometimes harmonize laws and regulations which, among other effects, make the costs of operating businesses in other countries more similar to those costs in the United States. An important noneconomic reason for establishing PTAs is to achieve foreign policy goals. Those goals include supporting the economies of U.S. allies and promoting the adoption of preferred domestic policies, such as environmental conservation or stronger workers' rights.

How Do Preferential Trade Agreements Work?

Preferential trade agreements facilitate trade and investment among member countries. To encourage member countries to trade, PTAs reduce or eliminate barriers to trade, such as import tariffs (taxes that countries impose on foreign-made goods), restrictions on trade in services, and other commercial rules that impede the flow of trade. In addition, PTAs facilitate investment among member countries by easing regulations on foreign investment and providing improved legal protections for foreign investors.

Preferential trade agreements also set commercial rules that, among other effects, narrow differences in the costs of operations among member countries. For example, some PTAs establish minimum labor and environmental standards and protections for intellectual property. If the costs of compliance are high, those types of rule-based reforms can impede trade and investment flows, making some businesses less competitive in foreign markets.

To ensure that member countries comply with the provisions of an agreement, PTAs establish dispute resolution mechanisms. Those mechanisms can take two forms: One provides a legal platform for countries to make claims against other member countries; the other enables investors in member countries to make claims against the governments of other member countries.

How Much Have Preferential Trade Agreements Affected the U.S. Economy and the Federal Budget?

In the Congressional Budget Office's view, the consensus among economic studies is that PTAs have had relatively small positive effects on total U.S. trade (exports plus imports) and, primarily through that channel, on the U.S. economy. The effects have been small because the agreements were mostly between the United States and countries with much smaller economies and because tariffs and other trade barriers were generally low when the agreements took effect. PTAs have had little effect on the U.S. trade balance (exports minus imports) and have slightly increased flows of foreign direct investment, mostly by encouraging additional U.S. investment in the economies of member countries. As a result, the indirect effects of PTAs on productivity, output, and employment in the United States have also been small and positive. Empirical estimates support that view. But those estimates are uncertain and may be understated, because the effects of nontariff provisions are hard to measure and because issues with data keep researchers from identifying how PTAs affect the service sector.

The effect of PTAs on the federal budget is unclear. In assessing the budgetary impact of previous preferential trade agreements, CBO's cost estimates have indicated that they would slightly lower the amount of federal revenues received from tariffs. However, those results did not consider how the macroeconomic effects of PTAs might alter the federal budget. Nevertheless, the small size of the effects on output suggests that the overall budgetary effects have also been small.

The Economic Effects of Trade on the United States

International trade contributes to the overall economic well-being of people in the United States in many ways. Without trade, people in the United States can consume only those goods and services that U.S. businesses can produce; some goods and services are unavailable, and the prices of others that those businesses are ill-suited to produce are relatively high. By increasing competition in the markets for tradable goods and services, increases in trade tend to raise U.S. productivity. Although trade expansion can reallocate workers across occupations, businesses, and industries, it has little effect on total employment in the long term. Higher productivity as a result of increases in trade tends to boost workers' average real wages and output.[2] With additional trade, people can consume goods and services at a lower cost. Lower prices for traded goods and services enable consumers to buy more goods and services—and a greater variety of them—with the same amount of income. Those same effects can also be seen in other countries that trade globally.

The benefits and costs of trade expansion are not evenly distributed: The costs are concentrated among less productive workers and businesses in all industries exposed to greater competition from U.S. trading partners. For example, laid-off workers in occupations that require less skill or in industries facing greater competition will experience spells of unemployment while they search for and train for new jobs. In a flexible and growing economy, most workers would be able to take advantage of a greater demand for workers in expanding sectors. However, in sectors, regions, and occupations with particularly weak demand for labor, workers could be unemployed for a long time. Some workers might permanently lose income or even stop working altogether.

Productivity

Trade can increase a country's productivity by reallocating resources to the most productive businesses within industries and by increasing the productivity of individual businesses.[3] The reallocation of resources occurs in both import-oriented and export-oriented industries.[4] Within all of those industries, increased competition from abroad pushes the least productive businesses to close.[5] In contrast, profitable new opportunities to sell abroad encourage the most productive businesses to expand and export.[6] That expansion also allows those businesses to take advantage of economies of scale and become even more productive. As a result, the average productivity of businesses within each industry rises, boosting the nation's overall productivity.[7] Over the past few decades, productivity in the U.S. manufacturing sector has improved substantially as competition from trade increased.[8]

Increased competition from trade encourages businesses to invest more in physical capital, improved production processes, and innovative techniques to remain profitable.[9] Closer trade relationships can promote the transmission of information and new technologies across borders.[10] (Some investments arise from such exchanges, particularly outside of the United States. Businesses' greater productivity from such investments may have contributed to the growth of overall productivity in global economies, especially for countries with less-developed economies.)[11]

Trade can also increase a country's productivity by reallocating resources to the industries within that country that can produce goods and services more cheaply than those in its trading partners. Trade encourages labor and capital resources to flow between industries to best take advantage of a country's natural resources, labor force, stock of physical capital, and technical knowledge. If resources are shifted from industries that are less productive to industries that are more productive, then overall productivity rises.

Total Employment and Average Wages

Trade expansion can have different effects on labor markets in the short term and the long term. In the short term, the competitive pressures from increased trade reallocate productive labor resources. Therefore, total employment can fall below its maximum sustainable level, at least temporarily, as workers who lose their job search for a new job.[12] In the long term, total employment should return to its maximum sustainable level as those displaced workers find jobs in expanding export-oriented industries and in other industries. However, the

maximum sustainable level of employment may be greater or smaller than it was before trade expanded. Insofar as greater trade raises average real wages, the maximum sustainable level of employment may be greater than before the trade expansion because changes in wages affect people's desire to work. In addition, to the extent that displaced workers cannot find new jobs over the long term, total employment may be smaller. Although it is difficult to estimate how trade affects total employment, the prevailing consensus in the literature is that, over the long term, trade expansion has had little effect on total U.S. employment and has raised workers' average real wages.

Output

In the short term, the effects of trade expansion on output can be difficult to discern. That is because the effects from disruptions surrounding the reallocation of resources may be greater than the effects from increases in productivity. But in the long term, by increasing competition and domestic productivity, trade generally boosts real economic output. Evidence from economic studies generally supports the claim that trade has contributed to the growth of economic output in the United States over the long term.[13]

Consumer Spending

Trade benefits consumers mainly by lowering the prices of some traded goods and services, which raises consumers' purchasing power.[14] When countries trade, consumers pay less for goods produced more cheaply abroad. But domestic consumers pay more for the goods and services that their country exports (because of higher demand from foreign consumers), partially offsetting that effect. In addition, domestic productivity growth and competition between businesses put downward pressure on prices.[15] Since the mid-1990s, relatively low rates of inflation in the prices of imports as a result of trade have increased consumers' purchasing power around the world.[16] Furthermore, low-income consumers in the United States have benefited more from trade than high-income consumers, because low-income consumers tend to spend a larger portion of their income on imported goods whose prices are more likely to fall as a result of trade—specifically, food and clothing.[17]

Trade also benefits consumers by increasing the variety and the availability of products.[18] Trade is an important channel for expanding the number of products available for purchase by domestic businesses and consumers.[19] That greater variety improves consumer welfare, although measuring the precise extent to which consumers benefit from more variety is difficult.[20]

Outcomes for Workers

Trade affects different workers in different ways. Greater trade benefits some workers, such as those employed in export-oriented industries or highly skilled occupations. But it harms other workers, who tend to lose income when they are displaced from their jobs for trade-related reasons. Estimating how many workers have lost or gained jobs from trade is hard because of the challenge of distinguishing the effects of trade from other factors that influence labor markets.

Some workers directly benefit from trade. As demand for labor rises because of trade in export-oriented or fast-growing industries and businesses, relative wages rise—benefiting those workers.[21] In the United States, another group of workers who tend to see their wages rise as a consequence of trade are highly skilled and more-educated workers whose services are in higher demand.[22] Similarly, those who work in occupations that require fewer routine or easily automated tasks are likely to see their wages rise as a result of trade.[23]

In contrast, trade can be costly for workers who become unemployed when their occupations, businesses, or industries shrink. In the United States, trade-displaced workers tend to work in industries subject to more competition from imports (such as the textile industry), relatively less productive businesses, or occupations involving easily automated or routine tasks (such as data entry or customer service). Those workers also are typically less educated, older, or longer tenured at their previous positions.[24] Most trade-displaced workers eventually find other jobs, but they are unemployed longer than workers who lose their job for other reasons.[25] In addition, trade-displaced workers tend to earn markedly less once reemployed.[26] Such workers who switch occupations when reemployed can lose even more income.[27] Even though most displaced workers eventually find new

employment, some workers displaced as a result of trade cannot, and they eventually stop working.

Attributing a lost or gained job to any single factor is difficult; for that reason, researchers have trouble determining how many jobs have been lost or gained from trade. Nevertheless, several studies have tried to estimate how many workers have been affected by trade. In one study, the Organisation for Economic Co-operation and Development examined all available U.S. data but could not precisely estimate the total number of U.S. workers displaced for trade-related reasons. The analysis suggested that although only a small share of job losses in the United States between 1997 and 2003 could be confidently attributed to trade-related factors, it is possible that increased competition from foreign firms was an important factor in a much larger share of all job displacements in the United States over those years.[28] Another study found that growth in U.S. imports from China from 1999 to 2011 may have led to significant U.S. job losses—accounting for nearly 10 percent of the decline in U.S. employment in the manufacturing sector over that period.[29] Researchers also have been unable to precisely estimate how many jobs have been created or how many workers have seen their wages rise as a result of international trade.

U.S. Trade Agreements

Trade agreements are treaties that stimulate trade and cross-border investment and set international commercial rules and standards. Since World War II, the major trade agreements have focused on lowering import tariffs and removing quotas on imported goods. Those large, older agreements—which had many participating countries—are known as multilateral trade agreements. In recent decades, however, the scope of U.S. trade agreements has narrowed to include fewer countries but has broadened to address other barriers to trade and investment. Those smaller, more recent agreements are known as preferential trade agreements. Recent PTAs have addressed other issues affecting international commerce, such as product standards and intellectual property rights.

Reasons the United States Establishes Preferential Trade Agreements

The United States establishes PTAs for economic and noneconomic reasons. By increasing trade flows, PTAs can help the United States and other member countries realize many economic benefits. In addition, trade agreements can be used to achieve foreign policy goals.

Economic Reasons. The United States establishes PTAs to realize the economic benefits of increased trade and investment. PTAs lower barriers to trade, such as tariffs and quotas, among participating nations, and they can increase cost efficiencies by specifying and unifying commercial rules and investment codes. In addition, the United States can use PTAs to promote the spread of free trade among all countries. As those agreements proliferate, countries not party to them will have greater incentives to either join existing agreements or negotiate multilateral agreements. Conceivably, the largest PTAs could expand or merge to eventually include all countries.

The United States establishes PTAs that try to harmonize laws among member countries which, among other effects mentioned below, can make the costs of operation in other member countries more similar to the costs of operation in the United States. One way in which the agreements do that is by strengthening labor and environmental standards in countries where they are weak. Imports from those countries tend to become more expensive as a result, whereas exports from countries with stronger standards, like the United States, tend to become more competitive in the markets of other member countries.

Noneconomic Reasons. The main noneconomic reason that the United States establishes PTAs is to achieve foreign policy objectives. By establishing such agreements, governments can support the economies of allied nations—bolstering the economic relationship between nations to possibly yield stronger political ties. PTAs also can serve as a valuable bargaining chip to attain foreign policy goals. The United States can offer PTAs to partner countries in exchange for adopting favored domestic policies—such as environmental conservation or stronger rights for workers. Furthermore, the United States can use the promise of becoming part of a PTA to obtain concessions or reforms from nonmember countries.

A Brief History of Trade Agreements

Several major agreements involving many countries helped expand trade from the end of World War II through the mid-1990s. Since then, only agreements between smaller numbers of countries have been ratified.

Agreements Involving Many Countries. In 1948, the United States and 22 other countries established the General Agreement on Tariffs and Trade (GATT) to formulate and enforce rules that govern international trade. A major focus of GATT has been to reduce barriers to trade on a nondiscriminatory basis. Before GATT, tariffs among countries were high, averaging between 20 percent and 30 percent.[30] By 1994, GATT had expanded to include 128 member countries, and most tariffs rarely exceeded 10 percent, especially among developed nations.

Trade liberalization under GATT is widely referred to as multilateral liberalization primarily because of the many countries participating in that agreement. A crucial element of GATT is the concept of most-favored nation (MFN) status. Under GATT, all members agree to grant one another MFN status, meaning that any favorable trade terms extended to the imports from any GATT member country must be extended to imports from all GATT member countries. GATT has been an important factor behind the substantial increase in global trade and has contributed to global economic growth since its inception.[31]

In 1994, the Uruguay Round of GATT negotiations established the World Trade Organization (WTO) to serve as a permanent forum for negotiating further trade liberalization and to monitor members' compliance. Because GATT reduced tariffs and eliminated quotas, multilateral trade negotiations under the WTO expanded to include rule-based reforms. Those reforms address legal issues such as investment protections, market access for trade in services, intellectual property rights, and labor and environmental standards. The WTO instituted those reforms to further facilitate trade and investment among its members by creating standardized rules for businesses operating in one another's countries. For example, in 1995, the WTO established minimum protections for intellectual property rights for member countries through the Agreement on Trade-Related Aspects of Intellectual Property Rights (commonly known as TRIPS). In addition, WTO negotiations in 1995 addressed liberalization of trade in services through the Global Agreement on Trade in Services. Perhaps most significantly, the Uruguay Round established a dispute-settlement mechanism that enables aggrieved countries to place punitive tariffs on the imports of countries judged to have violated the WTO's rules.

Table 1.

Characteristics of Partner Countries of U.S. Trade Agreements Before the Year of Implementation

Percent

Partner Countries	Year in Which Agreement Was Implemented	Cumulative GDP of Partner Countries (Percentage of U.S. GDP)	Share of Total U.S. Trade	Trade-Weighted Average MFN Import Tariff Rates of Partner Countries	Trade-Weighted U.S. Average MFN Import Tariff Rates
Israel	1985	0.7	n.a.	n.a.	n.a.
Canada	1989	9.7	19.9[a]	8.2[b]	n.a.
NAFTA[c]	1994	16.3	28.0	n.a.	4.7
Jordan	2001	0.1	*	18.9	2.8
Australia	2004	5.3	1.0	4.0	2.8
Chile	2004	0.9	0.3	6.0	2.8
Singapore	2004	0.9	1.6	*	2.8
CAFTA-DR[d]	2005	0.9	1.5	6.6	2.5
Bahrain	2006	0.1	*	5.6	2.4
Morocco	2006	0.5	*	19.9	2.4
Oman	2006	0.2	*	4.7	2.4
Peru	2007	0.6	0.3	6.8	2.4
Colombia	2012	1.4	1.0	9.1	2.6
Panama	2012	0.2	0.3	6.8	2.6
South Korea	2012	8.2	2.7	7.3	2.6

Source: Congressional Budget Office.

Data on average trade-weighted MFN import tariff rates come from the United Nations Conference on Trade and Development (UNCTAD) Trade Analysis Information System (TRAINS). The database contains historical data on tariff rates. For agreements with more than one partner country, the average among all partner countries is calculated by weighting each partner country's average tariff rate by the relative volume of U.S. exports to each country. Data on U.S. exports to partner countries that are used to calculate those weights come from the U.S. Census Bureau. Data on GDP come from the World Bank's World Development Indicators database. GDP data are in constant 2010 U.S. dollars. Dollar figures for GDP are converted from domestic currencies by using official exchange rates in 2010. Data on agreement implementation dates come from U.S. Customs and Border Protection.

CAFTA-DR = Costa Rica, El Salvador, Guatemala, Honduras, Nicaragua, and the Dominican Republic; GDP = gross domestic product; MFN = most-favored nation; NAFTA = North American Free Trade Agreement; n.a. = not applicable; * = between zero and 0.05 percent.

a. Includes only trade in goods; does not include trade in services.

b. Data for average trade-weighted MFN import tariffs for Canada are only available starting in 1989.

c. Includes Canada and Mexico. In 1994, NAFTA superseded the 1989 agreement between the United States and Canada.

d. CAFTA-DR was implemented by the United States, El Salvador, Guatemala, Honduras, and Nicaragua in 2006. Implementation of the agreement by the Dominican Republic and Costa Rica did not occur until 2007 and 2009, respectively. This table presents data for CAFTA-DR countries in 2005, the year before the agreement's initial implementation.

In the late 1990s, multilateral trade negotiations under the WTO began to stall. The Doha Round of negotiations began in 2001 but still has not concluded, even after several attempts to reach agreement. Global trade talks have proven particularly difficult in this round of negotiations because rule-based reforms tend to be more complicated and contentious than simply eliminating tariffs on industrial goods. For example, the WTO's negotiations to increase intellectual property protections have failed in part because less-developed countries are reluctant or unable to offer additional protections.

Agreements Involving Several Countries. Trade liberalization over the past few decades has shifted toward preferential trade agreements among a few countries spread over a broad area.[32] PTAs are a less effective method of increasing global trade flows than multilateral trade liberalization because, by nature, they include fewer countries—but that smaller scope has also made it possible to conclude negotiations. The United States has established more than a dozen PTAs in the past three decades (see Table 1). The largest PTA—as measured by the sum of members' real gross domestic product, or GDP—is the North American

Free Trade Agreement (NAFTA), an agreement among the United States, Mexico, and Canada that took effect in 1994. Apart from NAFTA (and its predecessor, the Canada–U.S. Free Trade Agreement between the United States and Canada), the United States belongs to 13 PTAs with 18 other countries.

Currently, the United States is pursuing two major PTAs: one with selected Pacific Rim countries (the Trans-Pacific Partnership) and one with member countries of the European Union (the Transatlantic Trade and Investment Partnership). For a discussion of those potential PTAs, see Box 1.

Provisions of U.S. Preferential Trade Agreements

PTAs generally include three types of provisions. The first type facilitates trade and investment by lowering import tariffs, easing quotas, and improving market access for service providers and investors. The second type sets commercial rules and standards. Although that type of provision also often stimulates trade and cross-border investment, its costs of compliance (if they are high) can impede trade among partners. The third type of provision establishes legal mechanisms through which parties can resolve disputes to ensure that partners satisfy the terms of the agreement.

Provisions That Facilitate Trade and Investment. Some provisions directly reduce the costs of trade or investment, and other provisions offer partner markets preferential access to goods or services. More recent agreements have included provisions that facilitate trade and investment by loosening regulations on services and cross-border investments. Among the topics that PTAs have addressed are the following:

- *Import Tariffs.* PTAs lower or eliminate taxes on foreign-made goods among trading partners, making it less costly for those countries to trade.[33]

- *Tariff Rate Import Quotas.* Under GATT, limits on how many goods can be imported from abroad were largely eliminated. Instead, those traditional import quotas have been replaced by tariff rate import quotas, which limit how many goods another country may import at a low (or zero) tariff rate; all imported goods in excess of that threshold are subject to a higher rate.

PTAs often loosen or remove those tariff rate quotas on imported goods from member countries.

- *Customs Procedures.* PTAs have streamlined customs procedures for imports from member countries.

- *Government Procurement.* PTAs have sometimes eliminated rules that obligate governments of member countries to buy goods and services from domestic businesses.

- *Market Access for Services.* Some countries protect their domestic service sectors from international competition by prohibiting foreign businesses from selling those services in local markets. PTAs can loosen those restrictions by granting service-sector businesses in member countries improved access to the local markets of other member countries.

- *Foreign Direct Investment.* Countries commonly restrict foreign ownership of domestic businesses in certain industries and regulate whether foreign businesses can open local branches or facilities. To encourage flows of foreign direct investment (FDI) among member countries, PTAs sometimes include provisions that relax those rules.

- *Investor Protections.* PTAs establish rules to prevent discrimination against foreign businesses that operate in domestic markets. By granting foreign businesses what is known as national treatment, those provisions reduce the risks that foreign investors face when operating in member countries.

Provisions That Set Commercial Rules and Standards. Some provisions that set commercial rules and standards can either stimulate or impede flows of trade and investment. They can impede flows if the compliance costs of the provisions make some businesses less competitive in foreign markets. Those types of provisions address the following issues:

- *Intellectual Property Rights.* Some PTAs establish rules that determine how long international holders of copyrights, patents, and trademarks may sell their products exclusively in member countries. Those provisions typically grant the intellectual property of foreign businesses stronger protections from domestic competition than were previously afforded.[34]

Box 1.

Potential U.S. Preferential Trade Agreements

Both the Trans-Pacific Partnership (TPP) and the Transatlantic Trade and Investment Partnership (TTIP) are intended to be comprehensive preferential trade agreements. As such, they lower tariffs and establish rule-based reforms among member countries. Those reforms would, for example, harmonize labor and environmental standards, protect intellectual property, and loosen regulations on international investment. The rule-based reforms are central to both agreements and are likely to generate the largest economic effects for the United States. Negotiations on the TPP concluded on October 5, 2015, but the President has not yet submitted the agreement to the Congress for ratification. Terms of the TTIP are still being negotiated.

Trade-Weighted Average Tariff Rates on Imported Goods for
Countries Negotiating the TPP and TTIP, 2013

Percent

Country	Agricultural	Nonagricultural	Overall
Australia	2.5	4.2	4.1
Brunei	0.1	1.7	1.5
Canada	14.2	2.2	3.1
Chile	6.0	5.9	5.9
European Union[a]	22.3	2.3	3.6
Japan	12.8	1.2	2.1
Malaysia	14.0	3.6	4.4
Mexico	26.6	3.3	5.0
New Zealand	2.3	2.3	2.3
Peru	1.7	1.8	1.8
Singapore	15.7	0	0.5
United States	4.1	2.1	2.2
Vietnam	7.3	4.9	5.1

Sources: Congressional Budget Office; World Trade Organization.

Tariffs are taxes paid on the value of imported goods. The trade-weighted average tariff is equal to the average of the most-favored-nation (MFN) import tariff rates set by a country, weighted by the volume of imports into each country (including both agricultural and nonagricultural products). More weight is given to products with larger import flows. MFN tariffs are the standard rates charged on imports from all members of the World Trade Organization, excluding preferential rates, or lower rates charged within quotas. The agricultural tariff is equal to the trade-weighted average of all MFN tariffs on all agricultural products. The nonagricultural tariff is equal to the trade-weighted average of all MFN tariffs on all nonagricultural products.

Tariff data are from 2013, the latest year for which such data are available.

TPP = Trans-Pacific Partnership; TTIP = Transatlantic Trade and Investment Partnership.

a. The European Union comprises Austria, Belgium, Bulgaria, Croatia, Republic of Cyprus, Czech Republic, Denmark, Estonia, Finland, France, Germany, Greece, Hungary, Ireland, Italy, Latvia, Lithuania, Luxembourg, Malta, Netherlands, Poland, Portugal, Romania, Slovakia, Slovenia, Spain, Sweden, and the United Kingdom.

Continued

■ *Labor and Environmental Standards.* PTAs have included provisions that establish minimum labor and environmental standards. Such provisions can improve the competitive advantage of businesses that already meet higher standards because they will face lower compliance costs.

■ *Phytosanitary and Sanitary Standards.* PTAs can establish rules for both plant (phytosanitary) and animal (sanitary) products.

■ *Data Transfer and Data Localization Rules.* More recent PTAs have tried to define rules regarding the cross-border transfer of personal data—specifically, how and where foreign businesses can store data on their customers and employees.

■ *State-Owned Enterprises.* PTAs have included rules intended to prevent governments from favoring state-owned enterprises; those provisions prohibit state-owned businesses from gaining competitive advantages over businesses from other member countries.

Box 1.

Continued

Potential U.S. Preferential Trade Agreements

The TPP is an agreement among 12 Asian and American nations (including the United States). It aims to reduce trade barriers and establish international standards and regulations for various economic and commercial issues.[1] The United States already has preferential trade agreements with about half of the TPP's member countries—but not with Japan, its fourth-largest trading partner.[2] If the TPP is ratified, Japan's inclusion would give U.S. exporters better access to a large and wealthy consumer market, which represents the TPP's most significant advantage for the United States. However, because trade-weighted average tariffs among the member countries are already so low (see the table), the rule-based reforms—not tariff reductions—are the mechanism through which the TPP would have its largest effect on the flow of trade among member countries. Those potential reforms cover many issues, including labor standards, intellectual property protections, regulations for state-owned enterprises, cross-border investment rules, and market access for foreign businesses in service industries.

The TTIP is a potential agreement between the United States and the European Union. Much like the TPP, the TTIP is expected to increase trade and economic integration as a result of rule-based reforms.[3] For example, unifying product safety standards across TTIP countries would reduce the costs that potential exporters face in trying to comply with disparate sets of product safety codes. Because average import tariffs between the United States and the European Union are already low, the lower tariffs stipulated in the TTIP would have less of an effect on the U.S. economy than the other terms of the agreement.

---

1. TPP member countries are Australia, Brunei, Canada, Chile, Japan, Malaysia, Mexico, New Zealand, Peru, Singapore, the United States, and Vietnam. South Korea has expressed an interest in joining the agreement after its ratification. For an economic analysis of the TPP, see United States International Trade Commission, *Trans-Pacific Partnership Agreement: Likely Impact on the U.S. Economy and on Specific Industry Sectors*, Publication 4607 (May 2016), www.usitc.gov/publications/332/pub4607.pdf (7.57 MB). Other researchers have also conducted analyses of the agreement. For example, see Peter A. Petri and Michael G. Plummer, *The Economic Effects of the Trans-Pacific Partnership: New Estimates*, Working Paper 16-2 (Peterson Institute for International Economics, January 2016), http://piie.com/publications/wp/wp16-2.pdf (2.43 MB).

2. In addition to the North American Free Trade Agreement (the agreement that the United States has with its two largest trading partners, Canada and Mexico), the United States has separate free trade agreements with four other TPP countries—Australia, Chile, Peru, and Singapore.

3. The countries of the European Union trade heavily with the United States. In 2014, the sum of trade flows from all European Union countries to the United States accounted for nearly 16 percent of all U.S. trade. By contrast, trade flows from Japan to the United States accounted for only 5 percent.

Provisions That Establish Dispute-Resolution Mechanisms.

PTAs also contain provisions for resolving disputes among member countries. Those provisions include the following:

- *State–State Dispute Settlement.* PTAs typically provide a legal platform for countries to make claims against other member countries for breaching a trade agreement.

- *Investor–State Dispute Settlement.* PTAs have included provisions that provide a mechanism through which investors can make claims against the governments of other member countries for breaching a trade agreement.

Effects of Preferential Trade Agreements on U.S. Trade

In all likelihood, most preferential trade agreements that have involved the United States have boosted total U.S. trade, but by relatively small amounts. The effects have been small because the agreements generally were with countries with much smaller economies than that of the United States and because the trade barriers before establishment of those PTAs were already low. Even NAFTA, the largest U.S. trade agreement (by share of U.S. trade) to date, probably only modestly affected total U.S. trade. Nevertheless, estimates of the effects of NAFTA and other PTAs are subject to considerable uncertainty, especially because they omit the effects of certain aspects of the agreements.[35]

The evidence also indicates that PTAs have not significantly affected the U.S. trade balance, because the small increases in exports and imports that have occurred have probably been similar in size.

Effects on Total Trade

PTAs can change total trade for a member country directly by creating new trade among all member countries and indirectly by diverting trade from countries outside the agreement. When trade barriers fall, exports and imports among member countries tend to rise because the goods and services that the agreement covers become cheaper and more readily available.[36] That change in trade sometimes comes at the expense of trade with countries outside the agreement—for example, imports from a partner country replace some goods previously imported from a country outside a trade agreement—a phenomenon known as trade diversion. As a result, the change in total trade among an agreement's member countries may be larger than the change in total trade among all trading partners.

The potential for a trade agreement to stimulate additional trade among member countries depends on many factors. Two of the most important factors are the relative size of the member countries and the extent to which PTAs reduce barriers to trade. Establishing a trade agreement with a much larger country (or a group of countries whose combined size is large) gives domestic businesses preferential access to a much larger market for their exports. For a relatively small country, that market access can significantly boost that country's total trade flows. By contrast, for a large country that establishes an agreement with a smaller country, the additional trade that the agreement creates is unlikely to be substantial in comparison with that country's existing trade flows. In addition, the greater the degree to which PTAs reduce barriers to trade among member countries, the greater the potential to increase total trade flows.

The effects of PTAs other than NAFTA on total trade have probably been insignificant, but such estimates are subject to considerable uncertainty and may be understated. Various issues prevent the models that researchers use from precisely estimating how PTAs affect trade flows (for more information, see the appendix). Those stylized and econometric models may systematically understate the effect of PTAs on trade flows, for two reasons. First, although most models of trade are well-suited to analyze the effect of tariff reductions, only to various degrees do those models account for how nontariff barriers affect trade flows. Second, because of modeling difficulties and data issues, some of those studies do not fully capture the effect of PTAs on trade in services—a group of industries for which the United States has a comparative advantage over most of its trading partners.

Agreements Other Than NAFTA. All of the preferential trade agreements affecting the United States, except NAFTA, have not had much potential to boost total U.S. trade. [37] That is because the United States has established PTAs mostly with significantly smaller countries or groups of countries (see Table 1 on page 6). In addition, trade barriers between the United States and its partner countries were already low. When partner countries signed agreements with the United States, average tariff rates on their exports to the United States never exceeded 5 percent, and (with the exception of Morocco and Jordan) the average tariff rates on U.S. exports to those countries never exceeded 10 percent.

Economic studies find that PTAs by the United States have raised total U.S. trade by small amounts, although magnitudes vary by agreement. For PTAs other than NAFTA, the increases in total trade for the United States have probably been insignificant (in relation to the existing volume of U.S. trade). In general, they have reflected small increases in trade with member countries, which have been partially offset by decreases in trade with other countries. Those findings come from the few studies completed before the establishment of those agreements that used stylized models of world trade to predict the probable effects of proposed agreements.[38]

NAFTA. The likely increases in overall trade from NAFTA are significant but still small. The findings for NAFTA are based on analyses done before NAFTA's establishment and empirical assessments completed afterward.[39]

Empirical assessments suggest that NAFTA substantially increased total trade flows between the United States and Canada, and the United States and Mexico, although the estimates of those effects vary greatly. A 2015 study reported the strongest estimates for the effects of NAFTA

Table 2.

Estimated Effects of NAFTA on U.S. Trade With Canada and Mexico

Percent

Study	Period Examined	Trading Partner	Growth of Trade Attributable to NAFTA	Total Growth	Share of Growth Attributable to NAFTA (Percentage points)
		U.S. Imports From Partner Country			
Caliendo and Parro (2015)	1994–2005	Canada	6.1	144.2	4.2
		Mexico	105.9	302.4	35.0
		Combined	32.4	185.9	17.4
Rimmer and Dixon (2015)	1992–1998	Canada	4.8	67.8	7.0
		Mexico	143.9	240.9	59.7
		Combined	41.4	113.3	36.5
		U.S. Exports to Partner Country			
Caliendo and Parro (2015)	1994–2005	Canada	10.5	104.8	10.0
		Mexico	127.8	180.1	71.0
		Combined	44.9	126.9	35.4
Rimmer and Dixon (2015)	1992–1998	Canada	16.9	63.4	26.6
		Mexico	27.9	77.6	35.9
		Combined	20.3	67.8	29.9
		Total U.S. Trade With Partner Country			
Romalis (2007)[a]	1994–2000	Canada	-0.3	62.5	-0.5
		Mexico	23.2	154.6	15.0
		Combined	6.0	88.1	6.9
Caliendo and Parro (2015)	1994–2005	Canada	8.2	125.7	6.5
		Mexico	117.0	240.6	48.6
		Combined	38.4	157.7	24.4
Rimmer and Dixon (2015)	1992–1998	Canada	10.6	65.7	16.1
		Mexico	81.8	153.5	53.3
		Combined	30.9	90.8	34.1

Source: Congressional Budget Office, using foreign trade data from the Census Bureau.

The studies cited in this table are Lorenzo Caliendo and Fernando Parro, "Estimates of the Trade and Welfare Effects of NAFTA," *Review of Economic Studies*, vol. 82, no. 1 (January 2015), pp. 1–44, http://dx.doi.org/10.1093/restud/rdu035; Maureen Rimmer and Peter Dixon, "Identifying the Effects of NAFTA on the U.S. Economy Between 1992 and 1998: A Decomposition Analysis," Global Trade Analysis Project (April 2015), http://tinyurl.com/gtap4657; and John Romalis, "NAFTA's and CUSFTA's Impact on International Trade," *Review of Economics and Statistics*, vol. 89, no. 3 (August 2007), pp. 416–435, http://dx.doi.org/10.1162/rest.89.3.416.

a. Includes only trade in goods and does not calculate changes to imports and exports separately.

on those total trade flows.[40] The results suggested that NAFTA accounted for about 34 percent of the observed growth in those trade flows over the 1992–1998 period (see Table 2). Two other studies found more modest effects.[41] All those assessments, though, suggest that NAFTA probably affected U.S. trade with Mexico more than it affected U.S. trade with Canada, primarily because more barriers to trade existed between the United

States and Mexico than between the United States and Canada when NAFTA began.[42]

Results from the broad literature on all trade agreements also imply that NAFTA resulted in a large increase in U.S. trade with Canada and Mexico, although the exact amount of the increase is uncertain. In a 2016 report summarizing the literature, the International Trade

Table 3.

Estimated Effects of NAFTA on Total U.S. Trade

Percent

Study	Period Examined	Growth of Total U.S. Trade Attributable to NAFTA	Growth of Total U.S. Trade	Share of Growth Attributable to NAFTA (Percentage points)
Romalis (2007)[a]	1994–2000	1.7	61.7	2.8
Caliendo and Parro (2015)	1994–2005	10.7	136.3	7.9
Rimmer and Dixon (2015)	1992–1998	4.6	62.2	7.5

Source: Congressional Budget Office, using foreign trade data from the Census Bureau.

The studies cited in this table are Lorenzo Caliendo and Fernando Parro, "Estimates of the Trade and Welfare Effects of NAFTA," *Review of Economic Studies*, vol. 82, no. 1 (January 2015), pp. 1–44, http://dx.doi.org/10.1093/restud/rdu035; Maureen Rimmer and Peter Dixon, "Identifying the Effects of NAFTA on the U.S. Economy Between 1992 and 1998: A Decomposition Analysis," Global Trade Analysis Project (April 2015), http://tinyurl.com/gtap4657; and John Romalis, "NAFTA's and CUSFTA's Impact on International Trade," *Review of Economics and Statistics,* vol. 89, no. 3 (August 2007), pp. 416–435, http://dx.doi.org/10.1162/rest.89.3.416.

a. Includes only trade in goods.

Commission found that PTAs "across the world have led to an increase of 30 percent to 114 percent in each partner's trade over a 10 year period after an agreement has entered into force."[43] Those estimates are varied and uncertain because of the difficulty in distinguishing the effects of PTAs from other factors that may have influenced trade flows over that time.[44]

Taking into account both the trade created among NAFTA members and the trade diverted from other countries, evidence suggests that NAFTA probably increased total U.S. trade slightly. Considering both those effects, analyses done before NAFTA began predicted that the agreement would slightly increase total U.S. trade (relative to the size of total U.S. trade with all countries).[45] Later empirical studies corroborated those predictions (see Table 3). According to one study, NAFTA was responsible for an estimated 7.5 percent of the growth in total U.S. trade between 1992 and 1998.[46] Over the longer period from 1994 (NAFTA's inception) to 2005, NAFTA's contribution to the growth of total U.S. trade was 7.9 percent, according to a second study.[47] A third study attributed only 2.8 percent of the growth of total U.S. trade between 1994 and 2000 to NAFTA.[48]

Effects on the Trade Balance

Estimates of the effects of preferential trade agreements on the U.S. trade balance are very small and highly uncertain.

By one estimate, NAFTA increased the U.S. trade balance by an average of 0.1 percent of GDP from 1992 to 2000.[49] Analyses of other preferential trade agreements find mixed results—some agreements have improved the U.S. trade balance and others have caused it to deteriorate—but in all cases, the estimated effect is small.[50] The reason is that economic factors besides PTAs (such as national saving and investment trends) primarily determine the balance of trade.[51]

Those mixed results reflect the difficulty in estimating how PTAs affect the balance of trade.[52] PTAs directly affect the trade balance through their influence on exports and imports; they indirectly affect the trade balance through changes in prices of goods and services, exchange rates, and interest rates.[53] Different ways of modeling those indirect effects can produce different estimates. In addition, many models that estimate the effects of PTAs exclude trade in services (a sector for which the United States has historically maintained a trade surplus). As a result, those models probably overstate the negative effect of PTAs on the U.S. balance of trade.

In any event, a country's trade balance does not have to rise for a country to benefit from a PTA. The benefits of lower prices and greater variety and availability of goods, for example, may outweigh the additional financing costs of a larger trade deficit.

Effects of Preferential Trade Agreements on Foreign Direct Investment

Although preferential trade agreements can affect flows of foreign direct investment in several ways, past agreements have primarily encouraged flows from more-developed to less-developed countries.

Three provisions of PTAs can directly affect FDI flows:

- *Lower Trade Barriers.* When barriers fall, exporting becomes less costly than direct investment, and FDI between member countries might decline as a result.[54] Lower barriers can also affect FDI flows from countries outside an agreement. For example, because of NAFTA, FDI flows into Mexico grew significantly as a result of foreign businesses' setting up affiliates in Mexico to take advantage of the preferential treatment of imports into the United States from Mexico.[55]

- *Stronger Protections for Foreign Investors.* Investment provisions can prevent discrimination against foreign businesses that operate in domestic markets—giving foreign investors national treatment.[56] For example, agreements have made it harder for governments to expropriate foreign investments, and they have relaxed rules that prevent foreign businesses in certain industries from opening factories or branches.[57]

- *Stronger Intellectual Property Protections.* Such protections include longer durations for copyright and patent exclusivity.[58] Countries with stronger intellectual property protections tend to have higher investment from abroad. Changes to such protections in past agreements have not been strong enough to significantly affect FDI.[59]

Preferential trade agreements also can affect FDI by signaling to foreign investors that a country, particularly one with a developing or emerging-market economy, is committed to domestic reforms. For example, Mexico's willingness to give FDI better protections under NAFTA signaled to investors the government's willingness to protect all international investments. For that reason, investors from countries outside the United States and Canada probably were more willing to invest in Mexico as a result of that country's commitment to reforms under NAFTA.

PTAs have probably increased flows of foreign direct investment from the United States to other countries

and, to a lesser extent, from other countries into the United States. That conclusion relies on results from studies that examine how all PTAs affect FDI flows, because economists have had trouble estimating how preferential trade agreements affect U.S. flows of FDI. Studies suggest that although PTAs increase investment flows between similarly developed countries, a much stronger stimulus of FDI flows is evident from developed countries to developing and emerging-market ones.[60] In addition, PTAs probably have increased the amount of FDI received by the United States. However, no studies of the United States specifically (to CBO's knowledge) have found evidence that PTAs have encouraged FDI flows into the United States, probably because it is difficult to distinguish the effects of PTAs from other factors that affect those flows.

Indirect Effects of Preferential Trade Agreements on the U.S. Economy

In CBO's view, the consensus among economic studies is that the small increases in total trade that have resulted from PTAs have yielded modest, but generally positive, indirect effects on the U.S. economy, increasing productivity, average wages, output, and consumer spending slightly. Nevertheless, those agreements have not had uniformly positive effects. Because PTAs encourage economic specialization, some workers and sectors have fared better than others.

Productivity

By boosting total trade between the United States and its partner countries, PTAs have probably promoted a more efficient allocation of U.S. resources and increased U.S. productivity in the same ways that trade in general affects productivity (as discussed above), although the size of those effects is uncertain. There is some evidence that productivity improved in countries that participate in trade agreements.[61] However, CBO was not able to find any studies that specifically estimate how much PTAs have increased U.S. productivity.

Total Employment and Average Wages

Most economic evidence suggests that the total number of workers directly affected by PTAs has been too small to significantly affect labor market conditions nationwide.

Most of that evidence comes from studies of NAFTA, the agreement with the greatest potential to affect U.S. employment. Those studies concluded that NAFTA's effects on the size of the labor market and net changes in total U.S. employment each year have been small.[62] Those findings are consistent with the economic theory that PTAs should have little long-term effect on total employment because all displaced workers would eventually find new employment or would have stopped working anyway. However, according to some estimates, NAFTA contributed to many lost jobs.[63]

Conversely, many U.S. workers have had some small benefits as a result of PTAs. By lowering consumer prices (primarily through their effects on prices of imported goods) and increasing the productivity of workers (from greater competition), those agreements have probably increased average real wages for U.S. workers, albeit only slightly.[64] If that slight increase occurred, it would have induced more people to work, increasing the U.S. labor supply to a small degree. To CBO's knowledge, there is no evidence of such an effect on the labor supply, although if it had occurred it would have been small and extremely difficult to detect.

Output

PTAs have slightly increased the total goods and services produced in the United States and have altered the composition of production across industries. By increasing competition and domestic productivity, PTAs can boost real economic output. As a result of the establishment of NAFTA, for example, annual GDP in the United States probably increased by a few hundredths of a percent, according to a CBO analysis from 2003.[65] In addition, a 2003 study by the International Trade Commission surveyed the literature and found that U.S. GDP probably increased by between 0.1 percent and 0.5 percent as a result of NAFTA.[66] The International Trade Commission and other researchers have estimated smaller effects on real U.S. output, stemming mostly from higher productivity, from the implementation of other trade agreements.[67]

By lowering trade barriers in the United States and other member countries, PTAs have slightly altered the composition of U.S. economic output. Typically, U.S. sectors that experience the largest gains in output after implementation of a trade agreement are those for which the agreement has significantly lowered trade barriers in partner countries. For example, research suggests that NAFTA led to output gains for U.S. agricultural exporters as a result of Mexico's agreeing to reduce strong import protections on corn and corn products. But other studies indicate that U.S. production of textiles and steel was lower as a result of NAFTA, because the United States removed import quotas on those products from Canada and Mexico. PTAs' effects on the composition of output are specific to each agreement and are generally small. Therefore, it is difficult to draw conclusions about how PTAs in general have altered the composition of U.S. economic production.

Consumer Spending

By increasing consumers' purchasing power (through lower consumer prices) and income earned domestically, PTAs probably increased total real consumption in the United States. According to some estimates, NAFTA boosted U.S. consumption by 0.4 percent between 1992 and 1998.[68] NAFTA also increased the variety and availability of Mexican products for U.S. consumers by offering Mexican producers wider access to U.S. markets.[69]

Outcomes for Workers

Preferential trade agreements have hurt some U.S. workers (sometimes substantially) and helped others. Workers in low-skilled occupations or in manufacturing industries have typically been harmed the most; those who lost their job usually endured the most substantial hardships. Many of those displaced workers experienced a costly transition to a new job, and most faced lower lifetime earnings as a result of that displacement.[70] Other displaced workers could not find a good match in a new job and stopped working. In addition, increased competition resulting from PTAs has stifled wage growth in certain occupations and industries, affecting even those workers who kept their job. For example, one study found that between 1990 and 2000, NAFTA decreased the cumulative growth rate of wages of low-skilled workers by 16 percentage points in U.S. textiles and plastics industries in comparison with the wages of similar workers in industries with no decrease in tariff rates under

NAFTA.[71] That study estimated that NAFTA probably depressed average wages for all workers (even those in the service sector) in the U.S. localities where businesses were most sensitive to competition from Mexican imports.[72]

Some U.S. workers have probably directly benefited from PTAs—particularly workers in occupations, businesses, and industries that have expanded as a result of those agreements—although the available empirical evidence is weak.[73] According to economic theory and analyses of other countries' labor markets, the nominal wages of those workers should grow faster than the wages of other workers because their services are in greater demand. Some empirical evidence supports those theoretical predictions, but no empirical studies (to the best of CBO's knowledge) estimate whether any U.S. workers have seen their wages rise as a direct result of PTAs.[74]

Effects of Preferential Trade Agreements on the Federal Budget

How PTAs affect the federal budget is unclear. Past cost estimates from CBO have indicated that PTAs, once implemented, would slightly lower federal revenues from tariffs.[75] However, those results did not take into account macroeconomic feedback—the estimated effects on the federal budget that would arise from changes in economic output or other macroeconomic variables.

Most PTAs have led to small reductions in federal tariff revenue, according to CBO's estimates. That revenue falls for two reasons. First, imports from member countries are subject to lower tariff rates. Even though imports from those countries increase under trade agreements, the associated boost in tariff revenue in the United States from greater volume typically does not offset the effect of the lower rates. Second, U.S. consumers replace imports from high-tariff countries with cheaper imports from countries with lower tariffs. Partially offsetting both of those effects is an increase in income and payroll taxes that stems from the lower tariffs (putting aside any effect on overall economic activity and income).[76]

The direct budgetary effects of PTAs on tariff revenue have been small in comparison with the total size of federal tariff revenue, according to past CBO estimates. In 1993, CBO projected that NAFTA would decrease federal tariff revenue by 2.6 percent (or between $2 billion and $3 billion) over its first five years, but the budgetary effects thereafter were unclear.[77] In 2011, CBO estimated that the Korea–U.S. Free Trade Agreement would lower federal tariff revenue by about 1 percent (or just over $7 billion) between 2012 and 2021.[78]

However, CBO's past estimates did not consider the ways in which the macroeconomic effects of PTAs might otherwise alter federal revenues and expenditures. By increasing economic productivity, output, and income, PTAs would probably increase federal tax revenues. The small size of PTAs' effects on output suggests that their budgetary effects would also be small, however, because budgetary feedback effects are generally a fraction of the effects on output.

As of yet, the economics literature includes no estimates of the effect of PTAs on the federal budget that take macroeconomic feedback into account.

1. See, for example, Richard M. Alston, J.R. Kearl, and Michael B. Vaughan, "Is There a Consensus Among Economists in the 1990's?" *American Economic Review*, vol. 82, no. 2 (May 1992), pp. 203–209, www.jstor.org/stable/2117401; and Daniel B. Klein and Charlotta Stern, "Economists' Views and Voting," *Public Choice*, vol. 126 (March 2006), pp. 331–342, www.jstor.org/stable/30026756. More recently, a 2012 Initiative on Global Markets survey of prominent economists found that 94 percent of the respondents agreed with the statement, "Freer trade improves productive efficiency and offers consumers better choices, and in the long run these gains are much larger than any effects on employment." See Chicago Booth, "Free Trade" (Initiative on Global Markets Forum, March 13, 2012), http://tinyurl.com/igm-chicago. Several of the respondents in that survey noted that society should do a better job compensating the workers and businesses that lose income as a result of trade.

2. According to a review of the research on the link between trade and economic growth, trade has significantly contributed to economic growth in the United States over history. See Scott C. Bradford, Paul L. Grieco, and Gary C. Hufbauer, "The Payoff to America From Globalisation," *World Economy*, vol. 29, no. 7 (July 2006), pp. 893–916, http://dx.doi.org/10.1111/j.1467-9701.2006.00828.x.

3. Within-industry reallocation is responsible for much of the productivity gains from trade. Two studies of the Canada–U.S. Free Trade Agreement found that such reallocation significantly raised productivity in the Canadian manufacturing sector. See Daniel Trefler, "The Long and Short of the Canada–U.S. Free Trade Agreement," *American Economic Review*, vol. 94, no. 4 (September 2004), pp. 870–895, http://dx.doi.org/10.1257/0002828042002633; and Alla Lileeva and Daniel Trefler, "Improved Access to Foreign Markets Raises Plant-Level Productivity... for Some Plants," *Quarterly Journal of Economics*, vol. 125, no. 3 (August 2010), pp. 1051–1099, http://dx.doi.org/10.1162/qjec.2010.125.3.1051. Another study found that within-industry reallocation accounted for two-thirds of the productivity improvements in the Chilean manufacturing sector between 1979 and 1986. See Nina Pavcnik, "Trade Liberalization, Exit, and Productivity Improvements: Evidence From Chilean Plants," *Review of Economic Studies*, vol. 69, no. 1 (January 2002), pp. 245–276, http://dx.doi.org/10.1111/1467-937X.00205.

4. According to some estimates, import growth may be important for spurring productivity growth. For example, see Jakob B. Madsen, "Technology Spillover Through Trade and TFP Convergence: 135 Years of Evidence for the OECD Countries," *Journal of International Economics*, vol. 72, no. 2 (July 2007), pp. 464–480, http://dx.doi.org/10.1016/j.jinteco.2006.12.001; and Francisco Alcalá and Antonio Ciccone, "Trade and Productivity," *Quarterly Journal of Economics*, vol. 119, no. 2 (May 2004), pp. 613–646, http://dx.doi.org/10.1162/0033553041382139.

5. Not all businesses profit from more open trade. Differences in productivity drive certain businesses to become exporters and others to exit the market when countries open to trade. See Marc J. Melitz, "The Impact of Trade on Intra-Industry Reallocations and Aggregate Industry Productivity," *Econometrica*, vol. 71, no. 6 (November 2003), pp. 1695–1725, www.jstor.org/stable/1555536.

6. One study found that increasing competition from trade in Taiwan (China) drove the least productive businesses out of the market. See Bee Yan Aw, Sukkyun Chung, and Mark J. Roberts, "Productivity and Turnover in the Export Market: Micro-Level Evidence From the Republic of Korea and Taiwan (China)," *World Bank Economic Review*, vol. 14, no. 1 (January 2000), pp. 65–90, http://dx.doi.org/10.1093/wber/14.1.65. Another paper found that through increased competition, trade stimulated a reallocation of resources from less productive businesses to more productive businesses. See Andrew B. Bernard and J. Bradford Jensen, "Exporting and Productivity in the USA," *Oxford Review of Economic Policy*, vol. 20, no. 3 (Autumn 2004), pp. 343–357, http://dx.doi.org/10.1093/oxrep/grh020.

7. Some studies present evidence for a possible third channel: reallocation across industries. One study found that type of reallocation from specialization accounted for a substantial proportion of the increase in productivity in Switzerland between 1997 and 2009. See Ulf Lewrick, Lukas Mohler, and Rolf Weder, *When Firms and Industries Matter: Understanding the Sources of Productivity Growth,* Working Paper 469 (Bank for International Settlements, October 2014),

www.bis.org/publ/work469.htm. However, another study found only interindustry reallocation as a result of trade. See Romain Wacziarg and Jessica Seddon Wallack, "Trade Liberalization and Intersectoral Labor Movements," *Journal of International Economics*, vol. 64, no. 2 (2004), pp. 411–439, http://dx.doi.org/10.1016/j.jinteco.2003.10.001. Another study found that workers take a long time to move to industries with a comparative advantage. See Naércio A. Menezes-Filho and Marc-Andreas Muendler, *Labor Reallocation in Response to Trade Reform*, Working Paper 17372 (National Bureau of Economic Research, August 2011), www.nber.org/papers/w17372.

8. One study found that the reallocation of resources may explain over 40 percent of the growth in the productivity of the U.S. manufacturing sector between 1983 and 1992. See Andrew B. Bernard and J. Bradford Jensen, "Exporting and Productivity in the USA," *Oxford Review of Economic Policy*, vol. 20, no. 3 (Autumn 2004), pp. 343–357, http://dx.doi.org/10.1093/oxrep/grh020.

9. The literature describes some such effects as dynamic effects. For examples of how trade can stimulate productivity improvements among businesses, see Alla Lileeva and Daniel Trefler, "Improved Access to Foreign Markets Raises Plant-Level Productivity... for Some Plants," *Quarterly Journal of Economics*, vol. 125, no. 3 (August 2010), pp. 1051–1099, http://dx.doi.org/10.1162/qjec.2010.125.3.1051; and John R. Baldwin and Wulong Gu, *Long-Term Productivity Growth in Manufacturing in Canada and the United States, 1961 to 2003*, Canadian Productivity Review Series Paper 2007015e (Statistics Canada, Economic Analysis, 2007), http://tinyurl.com/statcan-15-206-x. Also see Alla Lileeva, *Trade Liberalization and Productivity Dynamics: Evidence From Canada*, Economic Analysis Research Series Paper 2008051e (Statistics Canada, Analytical Studies Branch, 2008), http://tinyurl.com/statcan-11f0027mie; Johannes Van Biesebroeck, "Exporting Raises Productivity in Sub-Saharan African Manufacturing Firms," *Journal of International Economics*, vol. 67, no. 2 (December 2005), pp. 373–391, http://dx.doi.org/10.1016/j.jinteco.2004.12.002; and Jan De Loecker, "Do Exports Generate Higher Productivity? Evidence From Slovenia," *Journal of International Economics*, vol. 73, no. 1 (September 2007), pp. 69–98, http://dx.doi.org/10.1016/j.jinteco.2007.03.003.

10. One study found that technology spillovers caused by trade have significantly increased total factor productivity over the past 135 years. See Jakob B. Madsen, "Technology Spillover Through Trade and TFP Convergence: 135 Years of Evidence for the OECD Countries," *Journal of International Economics,* vol. 72, no. 2 (2007), pp. 464–480, http://dx.doi.org/10.1016/j.jinteco.2006.12.001. In addition, import growth has been shown to increase productivity. Another study found that increased openness to imports of capital goods improved productivity. See David T. Coe, Elhanan Helpman, and Alexander W. Hoffmaiseter, "North-South R & D Spillovers," *Economic Journal,* vol. 107, no. 440 (January 1997), pp. 134–149, www.jstor.org/stable/2235275.

11. For more information, see Hildegunn Kyvik Nordås, Sébastien Miroudot, and Przemyslaw Kowalski, *Dynamic Gains From Trade* (Organisation for Economic Co-operation and Development, November 2006), http://dx.doi.org/10.1787/276358887412; and Susan Stone and Ben Shepherd, *Dynamic Gains From Trade: The Role of Intermediate Inputs and Equipment Imports*, OECD Trade Policy Series Paper 110 (OECD Publishing, 2011), http://dx.doi.org/10.1787/5kgf17f17ks1-en.

12. Economic studies have established a connection between degree of trade exposure and job separations. See Lori G. Kletzer, "Trade and Job Loss in U.S. Manufacturing, 1979–1994," in Robert C. Feenstra, ed., *The Impact of International Trade on Wages* (University of Chicago Press, 2000), pp. 349–396, www.nber.org/chapters/c6198; Bernard Hoekman and Alan L. Winters, *Trade and Employment: Stylized Facts and Research Findings*, Working Paper 7 (United Nations, Department of Economics and Social Affairs, 2005), https://ideas.repec.org/p/une/wpaper/7.html; and David H. Autor and others, "Trade Adjustment: Worker-Level Evidence," *Quarterly Journal of Economics,* vol. 129, no. 4 (November 2014), pp. 1799–1860, http://dx.doi.org/10.1093/qje/qju026.

13. See Scott C. Bradford, Paul L. Grieco, and Gary C. Hufbauer, "The Payoff to America From Globalisation," *World Economy,* vol. 29, no. 7 (July 2006), pp. 893–916, http://dx.doi.org/10.1111/j.1467-9701.2006.00828.x.

14. That increase in purchasing power amounts to, in effect, an increase in consumers' real income.

15. Several studies looking at trade liberalization support the hypothesis that increased international competition puts downward pressure on domestic prices. For example, see James Levinsohn, "Testing the Imports-as-Market-Discipline Hypothesis," *Journal of International Economics,* vol. 35, no. 1–2 (August 1993), pp. 1–22, http://dx.doi.org/10.1016/0022-1996(93)90002-F; Ann E. Harrison, "Productivity, Imperfect Competition, and Trade Reform: Theory and Evidence," *Journal of International Economics,* vol. 36, no. 1 (February 1994), pp. 53–73, http://dx.doi.org/10.1016/0022-1996(94)90057-4; Filip Abraham, Jozef Konings, and Stijn Vanormelingen, "The Effect of Globalization on Union Bargaining and Price-Cost Margins of Firms," *Review of World Economics,* vol. 145, no. 1 (April 2009), pp. 13–36, http://dx.doi.org/10.1007/s10290-009-0003-8; and Jan De Loecker, "Product Differentiation, Multiproduct Firms, and Estimating the Impact of Trade Liberalization on Productivity," *Econometrica*, vol. 79, no. 5 (September 2011), pp. 1407–1451, http://dx.doi.org/10.3982/ECTA7617. However, one study found that after trade liberalization, businesses in India did not fully pass on to consumers the cost savings from increased productivity; see Jan De Loecker and others, "Prices, Markups, and Trade Reform," *Econometrica*, vol. 84, no. 2 (March 2016), 445–510, http://dx.doi.org/10.3982/ecta11042.

16. See Nigel Pain, Isabella Koske, and Marte Sollie, "Globalisation and OECD Consumer Price Inflation," *OECD Journal: Economic Studies,* vol. 2008, no. 1 (December 2008), pp. 1–32, http://dx.doi.org/10.1787/eco_studies-v2008-art4-en.

17. See Pablo D. Fajgelbaum and Amit K. Khandelwal, "Measuring the Unequal Gains From Trade," *Quarterly Journal of Economics*, vol. 131, no. 3 (August 2016), pp. 1113–1180, http://dx.doi.org/10.1093/qje/qjw013.

18. Results from several studies suggest that increased product variety is an important consequence of trade liberalization. For example, see Scott L. Baier, Jeffrey H. Bergstrand, and Michael Feng, "Economic Integration Agreements and the Margins of International Trade," *Journal of International Economics,* vol. 93, no. 2 (July 2014), pp. 339–350, http://dx.doi.org/10.1016/j.jinteco.2014.03.005; and Timothy J. Kehoe and Kim J. Ruhl, "How Important Is the New Goods Margin in International Trade?" *Journal of Political Economy,* vol. 121, no. 2 (April 2013), pp. 358–392, http://dx.doi.org/10.1086/670272.

19. One study showed that trade in intermediate inputs represents an important source of increases in product variety; see Pinelopi Goldberg and others, "Imported Intermediate Inputs and Domestic Product Growth: Evidence From India," *Quarterly Journal of Economics,* vol. 125, no. 4 (November 2010), pp. 1727–1767, http://dx.doi.org/10.1162/qjec.2010.125.4.1727. Another study found that trade was a large contributor to the increase in the variety of products in the United States between 1972 and 2001; see Christian Broda and David W. Weinstein, "Variety Growth and World Welfare," *American Economic Review,* vol. 94, no. 2 (May 2004), pp. 139–144, http://dx.doi.org/10.1257/0002828041301443.

20. For an example, see Bo Chen and Hong Ma, "Import Variety and Welfare Gain in China," *Review of International Economics*, vol. 20, no. 4 (September 2012), http://dx.doi.org/10.1111/j.1467-9396.2012.01056.x.

21. Several studies have found that trade raises wages for some workers. One study found that exports have a sizable positive effect on industry wages; see Philip Du Caju, Francois Rycx, and Ilan Tojerow, *Wage Structure Effects of International Trade: Evidence From a Small Open Economy*, Working Paper 1325 (European Central Bank, April 2011), http://tinyurl.com/itstheecon. Another study showed that an increase in exporting raised wages for skilled and nonskilled workers; see David Hummels and others, "Offshoring, Transition, and Training: Evidence From Danish Matched Worker-Firm Data," *American Economic Review,* vol. 102, no. 3 (May 2012), pp. 424–428, http://dx.doi.org/10.1257/aer.102.3.424.

22. See Catherine L. Mann, "How Does Trade Affect the American Worker?" in *Is the U.S. Trade Deficit Sustainable?* (Peterson Institute for International Economics, 1999), p. 59, http://tinyurl.com/piie-4iie2644 (PDF, 271 KB); and Ann E. Harrison, "Productivity, Imperfect Competition, and Trade Reform: Theory and Evidence," *Journal of International Economics*, vol. 36, no. 1 (February 1994), pp. 53–73, http://dx.doi.org/10.1016/0022-1996(94)90057-4.

23. One study showed that jobs with less routine tasks (such as communication-based occupations) tended to see wages for their workers rise as a result of trade; see Lindsay Oldenski, "Offshoring and Polarization of the U.S. Labor Market," *Industrial and Labor Relations Review,* vol. 67, no. 3 (May 2014), pp. 734–761, http://dx.doi.org/10.1177/0019793914067OS311.

24. Longer-tenured workers tend to have more job-specific skills that are less portable to other jobs. See Lori G. Kletzer, "Trade-Related Job Loss and Wage Insurance: A Synthetic Review," *Review of International Economics,* vol. 12, no. 5 (November 2004), pp. 724–748, http://dx.doi.org/10.1111/j.1467-9396.2004.00479.x; and Avraham Ebenstein and others, "Estimating the Impact of Trade and Offshoring on American Workers Using the Current Population Surveys," *Review of Economics and Statistics,* vol. 96, no. 4 (October 2014), pp. 581–595, http://dx.doi.org/10.1162/rest_a_00400.

25. See Jon Haveman, *The Effect of Trade Induced Displacement on Unemployment and Wages* (Purdue CIBER Working Papers, January 1993), http://docs.lib.purdue.edu/ciberwp/76; and Lori G. Kletzer, "Trade-Related Job Loss and Wage Insurance: A Synthetic Review," *Review of International Economics,* vol. 12, no. 5 (November 2004), pp. 724–748, http://dx.doi.org/10.1111/j.1467-9396.2004.00479.x.

26. Some estimates suggest that of the displaced workers most vulnerable to import-related job losses, approximately two-thirds earned less in their new job and about a quarter of those earned 30 percent less in their new job; see Lori G. Kletzer, *Job Loss From Imports: Measuring the Costs* (Peterson Institute, 2001), http://bookstore.piie.com/book-store/110.html. Another study showed that the losses suffered by workers displaced when companies moved operations overseas to take advantage of lower costs were significant—amounting to about half a year's earnings for those workers before they were displaced; see David Hummels and others, "The Wage Effects of Offshoring: Evidence From Danish Matched Worker-Firm Data," *American Economic Review,* vol. 104, no. 6 (June 2014), pp. 1597–1629, http://dx.doi.org/10.1257/aer.104.6.1597.

27. The wages of workers who switched occupations as a result of a trade-related displacement declined by between 12 percent and 17 percent; see Avraham

Ebenstein and others, "Estimating the Impact of Trade and Offshoring on American Workers Using the Current Population Surveys," *Review of Economics and Statistics,* vol. 96, no. 4 (October 2014), pp. 581–595, http://dx.doi.org/10.1162/rest_a_00400.

28. See Organisation for Economic Co-operation and Development, *OECD Employment Outlook 2005* (OECD, July 2005), http://dx.doi.org/10.1787/empl_outlook-2005-en.

29. See Daron Acemoglu and others, "Import Competition and the Great US Employment Sag of the 2000s," *Journal of Labor Economics,* vol. 34, no. S1 (2016), http://dx.doi.org/10.1086/682384; and Justin Pierce and P.K. Schott, "The Surprisingly Swift Decline of US Manufacturing Employment," *American Economic Review*, vol. 106, no. 7 (July 2016), pp. 1632–1662, http://dx.doi.org/10.1257/aer.20131578.

30. See Chad Bown and Douglas A. Irwin, *The GATT's Starting Point: Tariff Levels Circa 1947*, Working Paper 21782 (National Bureau of Economic Research, December 2015), www.nber.org/papers/w21782.

31. Between 1960 and 2014, global trade in goods and services grew from 25.0 percent to 60.2 percent of global GDP.

32. Despite the departure from the MFN principle, GATT treaties allow participating nations to join PTAs under certain circumstances.

33. Trade agreements prevent imports produced mostly by nonparticipating countries from gaining preferential treatment by setting rules for origin requirements. Those rules specify how much of the production process (or value added) for any imported final good must take place within member countries for a good to receive preferential treatment under a trade agreement. Strong rules make it harder for exporters in nonmember countries to use the tariff preferences granted under a trade agreement. Rules-of-origin requirements apply for all provisions of a trade agreement that provide preferential treatment to imported goods, not only tariff preferences.

34. In countries where intellectual property is granted stronger protection, some medicines can become considerably more costly for consumers; see Shubham Chaudhuri, Pinelopi K. Goldberg, and Panle Gia,

"Estimating the Effects of Global Patent Protection in Pharmaceuticals: A Case Study of Quinolones in India," *American Economic Review,* vol. 96, no. 5 (December 2006), pp. 1477–1514, http://dx.doi.org/10.1257/aer.96.5.1477.

35. Estimates of those effects are uncertain, for several reasons. First, data on trade flows are limited and often unreliable. Second, existing models may not fully capture the mechanisms through which trade agreements affect trade flows and economies. Third, researchers do not have reliable estimates of how nontariff barriers affect trade flows. The appendix discusses the sources of difficulty in assessing the effects of PTAs.

36. The rule-based reforms included in PTAs lower trade barriers and affect total trade, although their net effect is unclear. For example, harmonizing commercial standards can promote trade by making it less costly for exporting businesses to comply with various product safety standards in multiple markets. But standard harmonization can also impede trade if it raises production costs for businesses in member countries.

37. All other U.S. trade agreements have been with countries whose combined GDP was less than 10 percent of U.S. GDP. Even for NAFTA, the combined GDP of Canada and Mexico amounted to only one-fifth of U.S. GDP at the time of the agreement.

38. Before establishing potential U.S. PTAs, the United States International Trade Commission (ITC) employs a stylized model of trade to project the economic effects of those agreements. In those projections, the agency estimates that all agreements yield small increases to total U.S. trade. See, for example, United States International Trade Commission, *U.S.–Colombia Trade Promotion Agreement: Potential Economy-wide and Selected Sectoral Effects*, Publication 3896 (December 2006), www.usitc.gov/publications/332/pub3896.pdf (1.18 MB); and United States International Trade Commission, *U.S.–Korea Trade Promotion Agreement: Potential Economy-wide and Selected Sectoral Effects*, Publication 3949 (September 2007), www.usitc.gov/publications/pub3949.pdf (3.84 MB). Other researchers analyzing all recent PTAs (not just those involving the United States) also projected increases in total trade; see, for example,

Scott L. Baier and Jeffrey H. Bergstrand, "Do Free Trade Agreements Actually Increase Members' International Trade?" *Journal of International Economics,* vol. 71, no. 1 (March 2007), pp. 72–95, http://dx.doi.org/10.1016/j.jinteco.2006.02.005; and Christopher S.P. Magee, "New Measures of Trade Creation and Trade Diversion," *Journal of International Economics,* vol. 75, no. 2 (July 2008), pp. 349–362, http://dx.doi.org/10.1016/j.jinteco.2008.03.006.

39. For a review of empirical analyses of other effects from NAFTA, see Justino De La Cruz, David Riker, and Bennet Voorhees, *"Econometric Estimates of the Effects of NAFTA: A Review of the Literature"* (United States International Trade Commission, December 2013), www.usitc.gov/publications/332/ec201312a.pdf (124 KB).

40. See Maureen Rimmer and Peter Dixon, "Identifying the Effects of NAFTA on the U.S. Economy Between 1992 and 1998: A Decomposition Analysis," *Global Trade Analysis Project* (April 2015), http://tinyurl.com/gtap4657.

41. See Lorenzo Caliendo and Fernando Parro, "Estimates of the Trade and Welfare Effects of NAFTA," *Review of Economic Studies,* vol. 82, no. 1 (January 2015), pp. 1–44, http://dx.doi.org/10.1093/restud/rdu035; and John Romalis, "NAFTA's and CUSFTA's Impact on International Trade," *Review of Economics and Statistics,* vol. 89, no. 3 (August 2007), pp. 416–435, http://dx.doi.org/10.1162/rest.89.3.416.

42. The U.S.–Canada Free Trade Agreement, implemented in 1989, liberalized trade between those countries. NAFTA superseded that agreement in 1994.

43. See United States International Trade Commission, *Economic Impact of Trade Agreements Implemented Under Trade Authorities, 2016 Report,* Publication 4614 (June 2016), www.usitc.gov/publications/332/pub4614.pdf (3.39 MB).

44. An important complication of estimating trade creation from NAFTA is identifying the import and export growth that would have occurred without the agreement. Doing so is difficult in part because NAFTA began just as Mexico was growing rapidly as a result of policy reforms during the 1980s and early 1990s. Moreover, Mexico experienced a severe financial

crisis in 1994 that resulted in a steep depreciation of the peso, which encouraged exports from Mexico and discouraged imports to Mexico. An earlier review of NAFTA found that the agreement had a positive effect on the growth of trade flows between the United States and both Mexico and Canada, but that effect in the literature varied greatly for the same reasons. See Gary Clyde Hufbauer and Jeffrey J. Schott (assisted by Paul L.E. Grieco), *NAFTA Revisited: Achievements and Challenges* (Peterson Institute for International Economics, October 2005), http://bookstore.piie.com/book-store/332.htm.

45. For a review of studies completed before the implementation of NAFTA, see Mary E. Burfisher and others, "The Impact of NAFTA on the United States," *Journal of Economic Perspectives,* vol. 15, no. 1 (March 2001), pp. 125–144, http://dx.doi.org/10.1257/jep.15.1.125.

46. See Maureen Rimmer and Peter Dixon, "Identifying the Effects of NAFTA on the U.S. Economy Between 1992 and 1998: A Decomposition Analysis," *Global Trade Analysis Project* (April 2015), http://tinyurl.com/gtap4657.

47. See Lorenzo Caliendo and Fernando Parro, "Estimates of the Trade and Welfare Effects of NAFTA," *Review of Economic Studies,* vol. 82, no. 1 (January 2015), pp. 1–44, http://dx.doi.org/10.1093/restud/rdu035.

48. See John Romalis, "NAFTA's and CUSFTA's Impact on International Trade," *Review of Economics and Statistics,* vol. 89, no. 3 (August 2007), pp. 416–435, http://dx.doi.org/10.1162/rest.89.3.416.

49. See Maureen Rimmer and Peter Dixon, "Identifying the Effects of NAFTA on the U.S. Economy Between 1992 and 1998: A Decomposition Analysis," *Global Trade Analysis Project* (April 2015), http://tinyurl.com/gtap4657.

50. Most studies indicate that the U.S.–Korea Free Trade Agreement (KORUS) lowered the U.S. trade balance. Renan Zhuang, Jeremy Mattson, and Won Koo estimated before the agreement's implementation that KORUS would cause the U.S. trade balance to deteriorate by $7.8 billion, and the United States International Trade Commission found that KORUS would lower the U.S. trade balance by $362 million. See United States International Trade Commission,

U.S.–Korea Trade Promotion Agreement: Potential Economy-wide and Selected Sectoral Effects, Publication 3949 (September 2007), www.usitc.gov/publications/pub3949.pdf (3.84 MB); and Renan Zhuang, Jeremy W. Mattson, and Won W. Koo, *Implications of the U.S.–Korea Free Trade Agreement for Agriculture and Other Sectors of the Economy* (Center for Agricultural Policy and Trade Studies, North Dakota State University, October 2007), http://tinyurl.com/aer619 (PDF, 166 KB). The ITC has found similarly mixed results from several other U.S. trade agreements. For example, the ITC predicted that the U.S.–Australia Free Trade Agreement would boost the U.S. trade balance by $339 million over its 18-year implementation period and that the Dominican Republic–Central America Free Trade Agreement (CAFTA-DR) would raise the U.S. trade balance by $756 million over its 20-year implementation period. Conversely, the ITC concluded that the U.S.–Colombia Free Trade Agreement and the U.S.–Singapore Free Trade Agreement would reduce the U.S. trade balance by $66 million and about $108 million, respectively. Those estimates differ not only for economic reasons (differences in the size of tariff reductions) but also as a result of differences in the analyses' modeling techniques.

51. Trade deficits are not caused by either U.S. or foreign trade policies. Rather, they are determined by the balances between saving and investment in the United States and in other countries and the effects of those balances on international capital flows. Trade policy normally has little, if any, effect on the trade deficit because it generally has little effect on saving and investment, both domestically and abroad. See Congressional Budget Office, *Causes and Consequences of the Trade Deficit: An Overview* (March 2000), www.cbo.gov/publication/12139.

52. The ITC, for instance, warned in its study of KORUS that "simulation results should not be interpreted as changes in total imports and exports, or as implying meaningful information about the balance of trade impact of the entire U.S.–Korea FTA." See United States International Trade Commission, *U.S.–Korea Trade Promotion Agreement: Potential Economy-wide and Selected Sectoral Effects*, Publication 3949 (September 2007), p. xix, www.usitc.gov/publications/pub3949.pdf (3.84 MB).

53. Suppose, for example, that trade liberalization sharply increased U.S. agricultural exports. Greater agricultural output would raise GDP, which could lead to an appreciation of the value of the dollar. That change would tend to discourage U.S. exports and encourage more U.S. imports. The net result could be an increase or a decrease in the trade balance.

54. One study showed that the complexity of the production and distribution process often determined whether companies chose to serve those markets through exports (if the process was more complex) or through affiliates (if the process was less complex). See Lindsay Oldenski, "Export Versus FDI and the Communication of Complex Information," *Journal of International Economics*, vol. 87, no. 2 (July 2012), pp. 312–322, http://dx.doi.org/10.1016/ j.jinteco.2011.12.012.

55. One study found that NAFTA led to large flows of foreign direct investment into Mexico; see Maggie X. Chen, "Regional Economic Integration and Geographic Concentration of Multinational Firms," *European Economic Review*, vol. 53, no. 3 (April 2009), pp. 355–375, http://dx.doi.org/10.1016/ j.euroecorev.2008.05.002. More generally, Chen's results suggested that countries with relatively large labor pools and those that gained preferential access to large markets because of trade agreements were the most significant recipients of FDI inflows as a result of those agreements.

56. To ensure that all investment-related provisions are properly enforced, some agreements establish an independent authority to resolve legal disputes between foreign entities and domestic governments. When foreign investors have legal disagreements with domestic governments, dispute resolution authorities give those investors legal recourse outside the domestic court system. That mechanism reinforces the legal rights of investors and promotes additional direct investment in member countries. One study found that dispute resolution provisions in the U.S.– Vietnam Trade Agreement led to increased FDI flows from the United States to Vietnam; see Tim Büthe and Helen V. Milner, "The Politics of Foreign Direct Investment Into Developing Countries: Increasing FDI Through International Trade Agreements?" *American Journal of Political Science*, vol. 52, no. 4

(October 2008), pp. 741–762, http://dx.doi.org/ 10.1111/j.1540-5907.2008.00340.x.

57. As part of NAFTA, Mexico agreed to loosen regulations that prevented U.S. financial services businesses from opening branches or subsidiaries in Mexico.

58. In addition, agreements have tried to ensure proper oversight of the rules through a reliable legal system.

59. See Jeong-Yeon Lee and Edwin Mansfield, "Intellectual Property Protection and U.S. Foreign Direct Investment," *Review of Economics and Statistics*, vol. 78, no. 2 (May 1996), pp. 181–186, http://dx.doi.org/ 10.2307/2109919.

60. To CBO's knowledge, there is only one empirical analysis of the effect of U.S. trade agreements on FDI. Although that study found that NAFTA may have decreased total FDI among member countries, it could not identify how NAFTA affected FDI for each country in the agreement. See Philippa Dee and Jyothi Gali, "The Trade and Investment Effects of Preferential Trading Arrangements," in Takatoshi Ito and Andrew K. Rose, eds., *International Trade in East Asia, NBER–East Asia Seminar on Economics*, vol. 14 (National Bureau of Economic Research, August 2005), pp. 133–176, www.nber.org/chapters/c0193. Most empirical studies have found that agreements tend to significantly increase FDI among member countries. One study found that the stock of FDI among trade agreement partners was 27 percent larger, on average, than the stock of FDI among countries without agreements—an effect driven mainly by investment flows from developed countries to developing countries; see Eduardo Levy Yeyati, Ernesto Stein, and Christian Daude, *Regional Integration and the Location of FDI*, Working Paper 492 (Inter-American Development Bank, Research Department, July 2003), http://tinyurl.com/ iadb-wp492. Another study examined the trade agreements that created the European Union (the Europe Agreements) and estimated that FDI stocks between agreement members were, on average, 144 percent greater than the bilateral FDI stocks of countries that did not join the agreement. The rise in FDI among Europe Agreement members tended to flow from Western European nations to Central and Eastern European countries; see Badi H. Baltagi,

Peter Egger, and Michael Pfaffermayr, "Estimating Models of Complex FDI: Are There Third-Country Effects?" *Journal of Econometrics,* vol. 140, no. 1 (September 2007), pp. 260–281, http://dx.doi.org/ 10.1016/j.jeconom.2006.09.009. One other study estimated that trade agreements tended to raise FDI stocks among member countries by 170 percent above the levels of FDI that would prevail without those agreements over the first 10 years of enforcement. Like the other studies, those estimates reflect large increases in direct investments by developed countries in developing countries; see Max Büge, *Do Preferential Trade Agreements Increase Their Members' Foreign Direct Investment?* Discussion Paper 37/2014 (German Development Institute, September 2014), http://tinyurl.com/die-gdi-dp37.

61. Estimates from two studies indicate that the trade agreement between Canada and the United States improved the productivity of Canadian businesses; see Daniel Trefler, "The Long and Short of the Canada–U.S. Free Trade Agreement," *American Economic Review,* vol. 94, no. 4 (September 2004), pp. 870–895, http://dx.doi.org/10.1257/ 0002828042002633; and Keith Head and John Ries, "Rationalization Effects of Tariff Reductions," *Journal of International Economics,* vol. 47, no. 2 (April 1999), pp. 295–320, http://dx.doi.org/10.1016/ S0022-1996(98)00019-1. Another study found a significant positive effect of NAFTA on the productivity of Mexican businesses. See Rafael E. De Hoyos and Leonardo Iacovone, "Economic Performance Under NAFTA: A Firm-Level Analysis of the Trade-Productivity Linkages," *World Development,* vol. 44 (April 2013), pp. 180–193, http://dx.doi.org/ 10.1016/j.worlddev.2012.09.008.

62. Several studies emphasize that even though NAFTA created some jobs and destroyed others, the net effects of trade agreements on overall employment are insignificant compared with factors such as economic growth and technological change. For example, one study estimated that the job displacements in the United States associated with trade with other NAFTA countries between 1990 and 1997 (not identifying the specific effect of NAFTA) accounted for less than 2 percent of all U.S. job separations over that period. That study's authors, after incorporating their estimate of the number of jobs supported by new exports to NAFTA partners, concluded that

NAFTA marginally increased total U.S. employment. See Raúl Hinojosa Ojeda and others, *The U.S. Employment Impacts of North American Integration After NAFTA: A Partial Equilibrium Approach* (University of California, Los Angeles, 2000), http://tinyurl.com/ucla-ojeda (PDF, 361 KB). See also Mary E. Burfisher and others, "The Impact of NAFTA on the United States," *Journal of Economic Perspectives,* vol. 15, no. 1 (March 2001), pp. 125– 144, http://dx.doi.org/10.1257/jep.15.1.125; and Willem Thorbecke and Christian Eigen-Zucchi, "Did NAFTA Cause a 'Giant Sucking Sound'?" *Journal of Labor Research,* vol. 23, no. 4 (December 2002), pp. 647–658, http://dx.doi.org/10.1007/ s12122-002-1033-3.

63. A series of studies by Robert Scott and his coauthors had the most pessimistic assessment of NAFTA's employment effects. One study from that series estimated that trade between the United States and its NAFTA partners was responsible for around 92,000 jobs lost, on net, in the United States every year from 1994 to 2003; see Robert E. Scott, Carlos Salas, and Bruce Campbell, *Revisiting NAFTA: Still Not Working for North America's Workers,* Briefing Paper 173 (Economic Policy Institute, September 2006), www.epi.org/publication/bp173/. However, those estimates should be interpreted with caution, for two reasons. First, the estimates rely on an assumption that changes in the U.S. trade deficit can be translated directly into changes in employment—an assumption with little empirical support. Second, the estimates incorporate the assumption that NAFTA was responsible for all changes in the U.S. balance of trade with Mexico and Canada. Because several other factors influenced the trade balance with NAFTA partners over that period (exchange rates and economic growth, for example), the authors probably could not distinguish the effect of NAFTA from other factors that affected trade flows. For both reasons, Scott and his coauthors probably overestimated NAFTA's effects on U.S. employment. For additional commentary, see Gary Clyde Hufbauer, Cathleen Cimino-Isaacs, and Tyler Moran, *NAFTA at 20: Misleading Charges and Positive Achievements,* Policy Brief 14-13 (Peterson Institute for International Economics, May 2014), http://tinyurl.com/ piie-pb14-13; and Gary Clyde Hufbauer and Jeffrey J. Schott (assisted by Paul L.E. Grieco), *NAFTA Revisited: Achievements and Challenges* (Peterson

Institute for International Economics, October 2005), http://bookstore.piie.com/book-store/332.html. Another study found that imports from NAFTA were responsible for 10.7 percent of all job losses in the United States between 1993 and 1999. However, that estimate did not account for possible job creation from increased exports under NAFTA. See Lori G. Kletzer, "Globalization and American Job Loss: Public Policy to Help Workers," *Perspectives of Work*, vol. 6, no. 1 (2002), pp. 28–30, www.jstor.org/stable/23272039.

64. One review of the literature found that NAFTA raised average real wages in the United States, but only modestly. See Justino De La Cruz and David Riker, *The Impact of NAFTA on U.S. Labor Markets* (United States International Trade Commission, April 2014), www.usitc.gov/publications/332/ec201406a.pdf (135 KB).

65. For CBO's economic analysis of NAFTA, see Congressional Budget Office, *The Effects of NAFTA on U.S.–Mexican Trade and GDP* (May 2003), www.cbo.gov/publication/14461.

66. See United States International Trade Commission, *The Impact of Trade Agreements: Effect of the Tokyo Round, U.S.–Israel FTA, NAFTA, and the Uruguay Round on the U.S. Economy*, Publication 3621 (August 2003), www.usitc.gov/publications/332/pub3621.pdf (4.1 MB).

67. Analyses of other trade agreements done using stylized models also indicate small increases in U.S. GDP through those channels. For example, although the ITC completed no beforehand estimate of the effects of NAFTA on GDP, the agency's estimates suggest that KORUS, the U.S.–Colombia Free Trade Agreement, and the U.S.–Australia Free Trade Agreement had even smaller effects than CBO's estimate for NAFTA. See the following publications of the United States International Trade Commission: *U.S.–Colombia Trade Promotion Agreement: Potential Economy-wide and Selected Sectoral Effects*, Publication 3896 (December 2006), www.usitc.gov/publications/332/pub3896.pdf (1.18 MB), *U.S.–Australia Trade Free Trade Agreement: Potential Economywide and Selected Sectoral Effects*, Publication 3697 (May 2004), www.usitc.gov/publications/332/pub3697.pdf (1.81 MB), and *U.S.–Korea Trade Promotion*

Agreement: Potential Economy-wide and Selected Sectoral Effects, Publication 3949 (September 2007), www.usitc.gov/publications/pub3949.pdf (3.84 MB); as well as Congressional Budget Office, *The Effects of NAFTA on U.S.–Mexican Trade and GDP* (May 2003), www.cbo.gov/publication/14461.

68. See Maureen Rimmer and Peter Dixon, "Identifying the Effects of NAFTA on the U.S. Economy Between 1992 and 1998: A Decomposition Analysis," *Global Trade Analysis Project* (April 2015), http://tinyurl.com/gtap4657.

69. One study described how NAFTA increased the variety of agricultural products available to U.S. consumers. Examples of "new" produce include certain varieties of tomatoes and avocados imported from Mexico. See Cathy Jabara and Brendan Lynch, *Exports and New Varieties: An Analysis of U.S.–Mexico Agricultural Trade*, Working Paper No. 16 (United States International Trade Commission, 2006), http://go.usa.gov/xKpxM (PDF, 450 KB).

70. See David H. Autor and others, "Trade Adjustment: Worker-Level Evidence," *Quarterly Journal of Economics*, vol. 129, no. 4 (November 2014), pp. 1799–1860, http://dx.doi.org/10.1093/qje/qju026.

71. See Shushanik Hakobyan and John McLaren, *Looking for Local Labor Market Effects of NAFTA*, Working Paper 16535 (National Bureau of Economic Research, November 2010), www.nber.org/papers/w16535.

72. Ibid.

73. Workers in geographical areas whose economies have gained the most from PTAs may also benefit. Areas with businesses that expand as a result of those agreements see an increase in their demand for other goods and services to support the growth of those expanding businesses. As a result, service-sector workers in unrelated industries often see an increase in demand for their labor.

74. The economics literature has consistently found that exporting businesses tend to pay higher wages; for example, see Andrew B. Bernard, J. Bradford Jensen, and Robert Z. Lawrence, "Exporters, Jobs, and Wages in U.S. Manufacturing: 1976–1987," *Brookings Papers on Economic Activity: Microeconomics*, vol. 1995

(1995), pp. 67–119, http://dx.doi.org/10.2307/ 2534772. However, the literature has been unable to show whether exporting tends to raise wages or whether businesses that pay higher wages are more likely to become exporters.

75. For example, see these Congressional Budget Office publications: cost estimate for S. 1642, United States– Korea Free Trade Agreement Implementation Act (October 12, 2011), www.cbo.gov/publication/42643; cost estimate for H.R. 5684, United States–Oman Free Trade Agreement Implementation Act (September 22, 2006), www.cbo.gov/publication/18147; and cost estimate for S. 2610, a bill to implement the United States–Australia Free Trade Agreement (July 30, 2004), www.cbo.gov/publication/16161.

76. When import duties, excise taxes, and other indirect business taxes (such as fees on businesses) are lowered on goods and services, they tend to increase income for workers or business owners in the taxed activity and for others throughout the economy. As a result, revenues from individual and corporate income taxes and payroll taxes also tend to be higher. Increases in such indirect business taxes would have the opposite effect. See Congressional Budget Office, *The Role of the 25 Percent Revenue Offset in Estimating the Budgetary Effects of Legislation* (January 2009), www.cbo.gov/publication/20110. For the latest offset percentages, which vary annually between 25 percent and 26 percent, see Joint Committee on Taxation, *New Income and Payroll Tax Offsets to Changes in Excise Tax Revenues for 2016–2026,* JCX-7-16 (February 2016), http://go.usa.gov/xKpkT (PDF, 17 KB).

77. See Congressional Budget Office, *A Budgetary and Economic Analysis of the North American Free Trade Agreement* (July 1993), www.cbo.gov/publication/ 20868. In 2015, import tariff duties accounted for only 1 percent of all federal tax revenues.

78. See Congressional Budget Office, cost estimate for S. 1642, United States–Korea Free Trade Implementa- tion Act (October 12, 2011), www.cbo.gov/publication/ 42643. In addition, other CBO estimates of how trade agreements affected U.S. federal tariff revenues also have been small. CBO estimated that CAFTA-DR would increase the federal budget deficit by about $4 billion between 2006 and 2015, the Singapore– U.S. Free Trade Agreement would increase the federal budget deficit by about $1 billion between 2004 and 2013, and the Colombia–U.S. Free Trade Agreement would decrease the federal budget deficit by $22 million between 2012 and 2021. Those estimates incorporate the assumption that some trade will be diverted from countries outside those agreements in favor of countries covered by them. See Congressional Budget Office, cost estimate for S. 1307, Dominican Republic– Central America–United States Free Trade Agreement Implementation Act (July 18, 2005), www.cbo.gov/ publication/16993; cost estimate for H.R. 2739, United States–Singapore Free Trade Agreement Implementation Act (September 16, 2003), www.cbo.gov/publication/14758; and cost estimate for H.R. 3078, United States–Colombia Trade Promotion Agreement Implementation Act (October 5, 2011), www.cbo.gov/publication/42611.

Appendix:
Difficulties in Estimating How
Preferential Trade Agreements Affect an Economy

Estimating how preferential trade agreements (PTAs) affect an economy is difficult. Trade data are often limited and unreliable, and distinguishing the effects of PTAs from the effects of other factors is hard. Moreover, estimates of the economic effects of PTAs depend on modeling assumptions.[1]

Data Difficulties

Limited and unreliable data are major obstacles to accurately estimating the economic effects of PTAs. In particular, three types of difficulties are associated with data on international trade:

■ *Discrepancies in Measures of Trade Between Countries.* Trade partners sometimes report significantly different measurements for trade between their countries. One reason for the discrepancies is that countries typically collect data on import flows—from which they earn tariff revenue—much more carefully than they collect data on export flows, but even data on imports are often inaccurate.[2]

■ *Mistakes in Reporting the Origin of Imports.* Because today's business supply chains are global, goods often pass through a third-party country on their way from exporter to importer.[3] When that happens, the importing country is likely to attribute those imports

to the final exporting country rather than the original exporter.

■ *Difficulties in Measuring Trade in Services.* Because most services are not subject to tariffs, trade in services—which has been a growing fraction of overall trade in recent years—is not subject to the same reporting requirements as trade in merchandise. (Examples of services include financial services and telecommunications.) Therefore, governments usually expend fewer resources to collect data on services. Also, because services are often intangible, tracking those transactions is much harder than tracking trade in merchandise.[4]

Modeling Challenges

Researchers regularly use two types of models to estimate the economic effects of PTAs: stylized models of world trade and econometric models. Stylized models are based on economic theory and calibrated to real-world economic conditions. Using stylized models, researchers compare

---

1. For further discussion of approaches used to analyze the economic effects of trade agreements, see World Trade Organization, *A Practical Guide to Trade Policy Analysis* (WTO, 2012), http://tinyurl.com/wto-unctad12 (PDF, 2.28 MB).

2. Ibid. A recent paper describes the discrepancies between trade data released by the United States and trade data released by China; see Michael F. Martin, *What's the Difference?—Comparing U.S. and Chinese Trade Data,* Report for Congress RS22640 (Congressional Research Service, March 24, 2016).

3. For example, when buying a good from China, the United States records the full value of that good as an import from China. However, with the rise of global supply chains, most of that good's value might reflect value added in another country (such as Malaysia) before its arrival in China for final assembly. By attributing the entire value of the import to China and none to Malaysia, the United States overstates China's importance in trade and understates Malaysia's. As a result, researchers might incorrectly assume that goods produced primarily by a member country but assembled in a nonmember country (before final export) would not qualify for preferential treatment—when, in fact, they would qualify.

4. For more information on the challenges of collecting data for trade in services, see International Trade Centre, "Capturing and Utilizing Services Trade Statistics, A Guide for Statistical Compilers in Developing Countries" (no date), http://tinyurl.com/intracenorg (PDF, 266 KB).

two scenarios: one that incorporates the estimated economic consequences of the proposed agreement and another that does not. Those models offer some of the best available predictions of future PTAs' potential macroeconomic effects. Econometric models, by contrast, use economic data from member countries to estimate the consequences of trade agreements.

Both models have difficulties estimating the economic effects of PTAs, but for different reasons. For the North American Free Trade Agreement (NAFTA), for example, most stylized models predicted smaller economic effects from NAFTA before its implementation than the econometric models attributed to NAFTA after its implementation.[5] The main reason for that discrepancy appears to be that stylized models have underestimated the willingness of consumers to substitute imports from one country for imports from another.[6]

Stylized Models of World Trade

The stylized models, a class of computational general-equilibrium models, are grounded in rigorous economic theory and use estimates based on historical data as parameters.[7] They can assess the prospective effects of PTAs and thus are particularly valuable when policymakers consider the merits of possible agreements. The results of those models yield useful predictions of the sectors likely to expand or shrink as a result of PTAs. Stylized models also predict how lower tariffs are likely to affect

trade among member countries and between a member country and the rest of the world.

Although stylized models can evaluate the mechanisms by which PTAs promote specialization and alter trade flows, their quantitative predictions should be interpreted with caution. Stylized models of world trade have difficulty capturing the effects of nontariff provisions—such as labor standards and intellectual property protections—on trade flows. The structure of stylized models requires researchers to convert all nontariff provisions associated with a trade agreement into an equivalent tariff reduction on specific goods or services. In other words, all nontariff provisions need to be described in the model as if those provisions affected prices systematically.[8] However, some effects of nontariff provisions cannot be represented appropriately as a change in tariff rates, making it hard for those models to capture the economic effects of those nontariff provisions.[9] Therefore, that required conversion adds another layer of uncertainty to quantitative estimates of PTAs' economic effects. Furthermore, the results from such models are particularly sensitive to estimates of how consumers would substitute imports from one country for the imports of another if the relative prices of those imports changed. Because those estimates vary widely, assessments of the economic impact of changes in trade policy also vary considerably, making it important to check the robustness of the results to changes in those parameters.[10] In addition, stylized models often have difficulty capturing the costs that occur when trade agreements reallocate economic resources. For example, those models typically do not estimate the

---

5. See Timothy J. Kehoe, *An Evaluation of the Performance of Applied General Equilibrium Models of the Impact of NAFTA*, Staff Report 320 (Federal Reserve Bank of Minneapolis, August 2003), http://tinyurl.com/minneapolis-fed-sr320; and Serge Shikher, "Predicting the Effects of NAFTA: Now We Can Do It Better!" *Journal of International and Global Economic Studies,* vol. 5, no. 2 (December 2012), pp. 32–59, http://tinyurl.com/shikher2012 (PDF, 497 KB).

6. See Serge Shikher, "Predicting the Effects of NAFTA: Now We Can Do It Better!" *Journal of International and Global Economic Studies,* vol. 5, no. 2 (December 2012), pp. 32–59, http://tinyurl.com/shikher2012 (PDF, 497 KB).

7. Computational general-equilibrium models are used to analyze economic behavioral relationships and interactions among all sectors of an economy—households, businesses, and governments—in ways that are consistent with economic theory. Stylized models of world trade are used to analyze economic behavioral relationships and relationships among all major trading nations. Such models allow analysts to use historical data to simulate how those sectors would react to a potential change in trade policy and how those reactions might alter macroeconomic variables.

8. A recent study documents difficulties in estimating how trade policies lower trade costs. The authors emphasize the issues researchers confront when trying to estimate the extent to which nontariff barriers affect trade costs. See Pinelopi K. Goldberg and Nina Pavcnik, *The Effects of Trade Policy,* Working Paper 21957 (National Bureau of Economic Research, February 2016), www.nber.org/papers/w21957.

9. This is particularly true for market access provisions in service sectors. Trade agreements sometimes include provisions that allow businesses in service sectors to more easily sell their services to domestic businesses and consumers in member countries. Such reforms have complex and potentially substantial effects on both trade in services and investment flows between member countries, but distilling those effects into a measure of an equivalent reduction in tariff rates on those services is challenging.

10. For more discussion, see World Trade Organization, *A Practical Guide to Trade Policy Analysis* (WTO, 2012), http://tinyurl.com/wto-unctad12 (PDF, 2.28 MB).

transition costs borne by workers whose jobs get displaced by the agreement.[11] As a result, estimates from stylized models may understate the costs of establishing trade agreements.

Researchers use stylized models to assess PTAs in two ways, and each method has drawbacks. One way highlights how an economy would differ if a trade agreement was fully implemented immediately. The other way projects economic conditions in some future year (or years), typically in the year when a trade agreement is likely to be fully established (usually 10 years or 15 years after the agreement takes effect). Analyses that assume immediate implementation can offer insight into economic relationships and the general direction of the effects of PTAs on certain economic variables. But such analyses are much less likely to reliably estimate the size of the effects, because PTAs take years to implement. By contrast, analyses that project future effects of PTAs can be problematic because they depend on the underlying economic forecast, which is uncertain.

Econometric Models

Once a trade agreement has been in effect for several years, researchers can use newly collected data and

econometric models to estimate its economic effects. Those models are particularly useful for learning how previously implemented PTAs have affected economies. Although econometric models are also grounded in economic theory, they require fewer structural assumptions than stylized models of world trade. Furthermore, econometric analyses can be used to estimate more detailed effects of PTAs than most stylized models.

The results of such analyses must be interpreted with caution, however. Econometric models cannot easily separate the effect of PTAs from unobserved or unmeasurable factors that may affect the economies of member countries. Econometric models have difficulties capturing the indirect macroeconomic effects of changes in trade policy. In addition, estimated effects from econometric models are susceptible to certain biases in the data. For example, countries that enter into PTAs differ systematically from countries that do not. If econometric models do not control for the factors that make countries more or less likely to enter into PTAs, that source of bias might distort the estimated effects of those agreements.[12]

---

11. See David Riker and William Swanson, *A Survey of Empirical Models of Labor Transitions Following Trade Liberalization* (United States International Trade Commission, September 2015), www.usitc.gov/publications/332/ec201406a.pdf (224 KB).

12. If models neglect to account for those factors, they are likely to significantly underestimate the effects of trade agreements on trade flows. See Scott L. Baier and Jeffrey H. Bergstrand, "Do Free Trade Agreements Actually Increase Members' International Trade?" *Journal of International Economics,* vol. 71, no. 1 (March 2007), pp. 72–95, http://dx.doi.org/10.1016/j.jinteco.2006.02.005.

About This Document

This Congressional Budget Office report was prepared at the request of the Chairman of the House Ways and Means Committee. In keeping with CBO's mandate to provide objective, impartial analysis, this report makes no recommendations.

Daniel Fried wrote the report, with guidance from Jeffrey Werling and Kim Kowalewski. Mark Booth, Ann Futrell, Mark Hadley, Joseph Kile, Nathan Musick, and Charles Whalen provided useful comments and suggestions on various drafts of the report. Robert Shackleton, Claire Sleigh, and Adam Staveski fact-checked the report.

Helpful comments were also provided by Scott Baier of Clemson University; Jeffrey Bergstrand of the University of Notre Dame; Maggie Chen of the George Washington University; Gary Hufbauer of the Peterson Institute for International Economics; Nuno Limão of the University of Maryland; John McLaren of the University of Virginia; Nina Pavcnik of Dartmouth College; and Dani Rodrik of Harvard University. The assistance of external reviewers implies no responsibility for the final product, which rests solely with CBO.

Wendy Edelberg and Jeffrey Kling reviewed the report, Christine Bogusz and Gabe Waggoner edited it, and Jeanine Rees prepared it for publication. Maureen Costantino designed the cover. An electronic version is available on CBO's website (www.cbo.gov/publication/51924).

Keith Hall
Director

September 2016